A SELECT LIBRARY

OF THE

NICENE AND POST-NICENE FATHERS

OF

THE CHRISTIAN CHURCH

EDITED BY

PHILIP SCHAFF, D.D., LL.D.,

PROFESSOR OF CHURCH HISTORY IN THE UNION THEOLOGICAL SEMINARY, NEW YORK

IN CONNECTION WITH A NUMBER OF PATRISTIC SCHOLARS OF EUROPE
AND AMERICA

VOLUME IX

SAINT CHRYSOSTOM:

ON THE PRIESTHOOD; ASCETIC TREATISES; SELECT HOMILIES
AND LETTERS; HOMILIES ON THE STATUES

T&T CLARK
EDINBURGH

WM. B. EERDMANS PUBLISHING COMPANY
GRAND RAPIDS, MICHIGAN

British Library Cataloguing in Publication Data

Nicene & Post-Nicene Fathers. — 1st series
1. Fathers of the church
I. Title   II. Schaff, Philip
230'.11   BR60.A62

T&T Clark ISBN 0 567 09398 0

Eerdmans ISBN 0-8028-8107-6

Reprinted, May 1989

PHOTOLITHOPRINTED BY EERDMANS PRINTING COMPANY
GRAND RAPIDS, MICHIGAN, UNITED STATES OF AMERICA